W9-CQW-129

Animal Classification

Fish

by Erica Donner

Bullfrog
Books

Ideas for Parents and Teachers

Bullfrog Books let children practice reading informational text at the earliest reading levels. Repetition, familiar words, and photo labels support early readers.

Before Reading

- Discuss the cover photo. What does it tell them?

- Look at the picture glossary together. Read and discuss the words.

Read the Book

- "Walk" through the book and look at the photos. Let the child ask questions. Point out the photo labels.

- Read the book to the child, or have him or her read independently.

After Reading

- Prompt the child to think more. Ask: What different kinds of fish have you seen before?

Bullfrog Books are published by Jump!
5357 Penn Avenue South
Minneapolis, MN 55419
www.jumplibrary.com

Library of Congress Cataloging-in-Publication Data

Names: Donner, Erica, author.
Title: Fish / by Erica Donner.
Description: Minneapolis, MN: Jump!, Inc., 2016.
Series: Animal classification
Series: Bullfrog books | Includes index.
Audience: Ages 5 to 8. | Audience: Grades K to 3.
Identifiers: LCCN 2016038715 (print)
LCCN 2016039933 (ebook)
ISBN 9781620315385 (hard cover: alk. paper)
ISBN 9781620315927 (pbk.)
ISBN 9781624964817 (e-book)
Subjects: LCSH: Fishes—Juvenile literature.
Classification: LCC QL617.2 .D66 2016 (print)
LCC QL617.2 (ebook) | DDC 597—dc23
LC record available at https://lccn.loc.gov/2016038715

Editor: Kirsten Chang
Book Designer: Molly Ballanger
Photo Researcher: Molly Ballanger

Photo Credits: All photos by Shutterstock except: Alamy, 5, 12–13, 14–15, 18, 23br; Getty, 8–9; iStock, 6–7; National Geographic Creative, 16–17.

Printed in the United States of America at Corporate Graphics in North Mankato, Minnesota.

Table of Contents

Look! What is that?

A bass!

A bass is a kind of fish.

What makes a fish?

Fish live in water.

gills

Fish have gills.
They let fish breathe
underwater.

Fish have fins.
They help fish swim.

fin

Fish have scales. They protect their bodies.

scales

Fish have a backbone.

It keeps their
spinal cord safe.

backbone

13

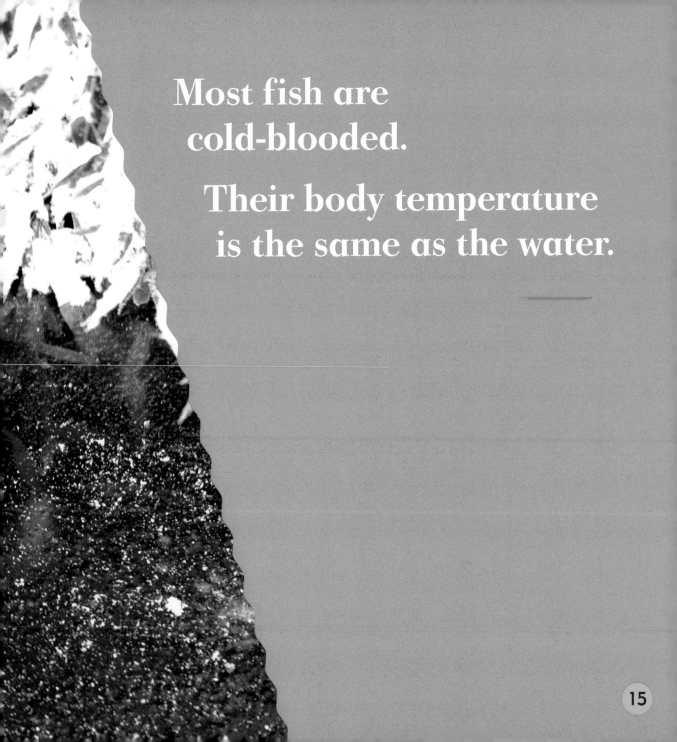

Most fish are
cold-blooded.

Their body temperature
is the same as the water.

Most fish lay eggs.

Wow! Look at
all the eggs.

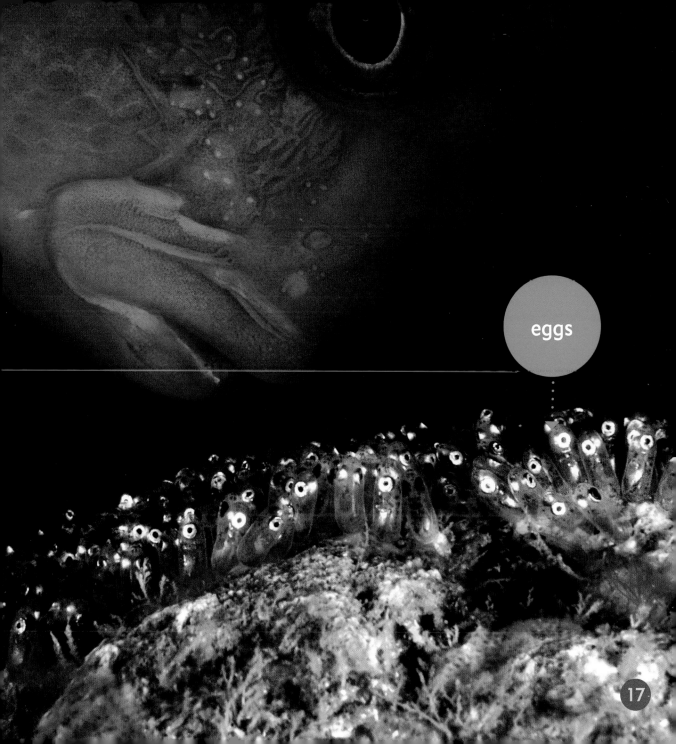

eggs

17

Some fish are huge.

A whale shark is a fish.

Some fish are small.
A goldfish is a fish, too.

Fish are cool!

What Makes a Fish?

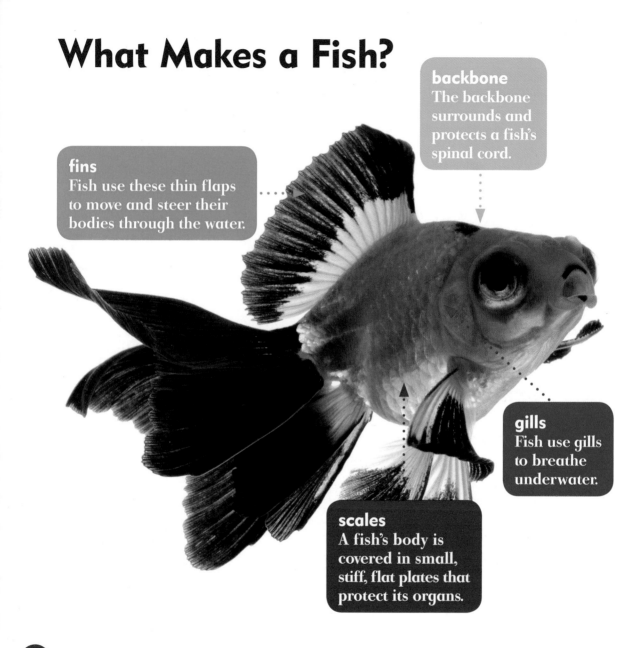

backbone
The backbone surrounds and protects a fish's spinal cord.

fins
Fish use these thin flaps to move and steer their bodies through the water.

gills
Fish use gills to breathe underwater.

scales
A fish's body is covered in small, stiff, flat plates that protect its organs.

Picture Glossary

cold-blooded
Having a body temperature that changes with the surroundings.

spinal cord
The cord of nervous tissue that carries messages to and from the brain.

protect
To cover or shield from something that would destroy or injure.

whale shark
The largest known fish, growing to a length of up to 40 feet (12 meters).

Index

To Learn More

Learning more is as easy as 1, 2, 3.

1) Go to www.factsurfer.com

2) Enter "fish" into the search box.

3) Click the "Surf" button to see a list of websites.

With factsurfer.com, finding more information is just a click away.